District Learning Action Cell (DsLAC):
Intervention for Teachers' Apprehension to Teach Practical Research

Cerelo B. Abasolo

DepED ROVII–Policy, Planning, and Research Division

Leavitt Peak Press

ISBN: 978-1-967361-08-3 (sc)
ISBN: 978-1-967361-09-0 (e)

Rev. date: 04/02/2025

An Action Research Proposal
Presented to the

Regional Research Committee (RRC)
For
Non-BERF
2024

District Learning Action Cell (DsLAC): Intervention for Teachers' Apprehension to Teach Practical Research

Cerelo B. Abasolo
Cerelo.abasolo@deped.gov.ph
Teacher III-Sangat National High School

CONTENTS

ABSTRACT

This study investigates the effect of the District Learning Action Cell (DsLAC) as an intervention to address teachers' apprehensions about teaching practical research. Employing a qualitative group case design, the research aims to evaluate the effect of DsLAC on teachers' readiness to teach practical research subjects. The central problem addressed is how the implementation of DsLAC contributes to reducing teachers' apprehensions regarding practical research instruction. The results reveal a significant improvement in teachers' confidence and competence in delivering practical research content after participating in the DsLAC program. The discussion highlights the positive influence of collaborative learning and professional development opportunities provided by DsLAC on enhancing teachers' pedagogical skills. The findings underscore the value of targeted interventions like DsLAC in improving teacher preparedness and instructional quality in practical research education. The study concludes that DsLAC effectively mitigates teachers' apprehensions and recommends further integration of similar interventions to support educators in effectively teaching practical research subjects

Keywords : *Practical research , teaching strategy, district action Cell (DsLAC) descriptive research design, Sangat National high school, San Fernando II, Cebu, action research.*

ACKNOWLEDGMENT

The researcher wishes to express his deepest thanks and heartfelt gratitude to the people who have generously shared and extended their expertise, efforts, and their priceless contributions in carrying out this study. The researcher would like to express his special gratitude and appreciation to the following people who contributed a lot to this study:

Jenelyn V. Craste, public school district supervisor-San Fernando II, for allowing

the researcher to conduct the action research study and for making the research comfortable on the day of his defense;

Dr. Apple Maye Susvilla- Barabat, Cebu province senior program specialist, in

research, for her constructive criticisms, ideas, and corrections from research proposal development to final report write-up of this study;

Dr. Nanette D. Yamlay, Principal II, Sangat National High School, who had always been helpful and cooperative during the conduct of the stand, giving her idea and support to help me achieve my goal;

The researcher's son, Iua Jhelo B. Abasolo, who understood the time spent away from him during Saturdays and Sundays;

Cebu Province Division Personnel, for the support of the teachers in making the action research to their respective station.

Researcher's friend in Sangat NHS family and the senior high school teachers in San Fernando District II, who assisted the researcher in giving information and acted sometimes as the researcher's sounding board; and

Finally, and most importantly, to Almighty God for giving him the strength, good health, and wisdom to do this work successfully. May the grace of the Lord be with us all.

THE RESEARCHER

Chapter 1

Introduction

Context and Rationale

Every educational institution shares the common objective of pursuing the highest caliber of teachers, as they firmly believe that the quality of instruction significantly impacts the overall quality of learning. The Department of Education strongly emphasizes the importance of professional development interventions and recognizes the critical role of teacher capacity building. However, the noble goal of education faces a major obstacle in some schools because some teachers lack confidence and are apprehensive about teaching, especially when it comes to practical research subjects. Embracing the District Learning Action Cell approach, the San Fernando II District Research Coordinator come up with an innovative resolution for this issue. Through the implementation of this approach, teachers in San Fernando District II will receive the necessary assistance and resources to proficiently teach practical research subjects.

In line with this, Valdehueza et al. (2020) emphasize the crucial role of effective teachers in enhancing the education system and increasing learning standard. It was suggested that Education Supervisors consistently provide the Learning Action Cell (LAC) as top priority and take into account the suggested activities to further integrate 21st century capabilities. By putting the Learning Action Cell instructional designs into practice, teachers may optimize the advantages of cooperation among educators. According to DepEd Order No. 35, s. 2016, a Learning Action Cell was defined as a group of educators working together during learning sessions under the direction of the school principal or a designated LAC Leader to solve shared concerns.

One significant issue at San Fernando District II is that some teachers expressed their fear and hesitation about teaching practical research during the focus group discussion. Their lack of knowledge and practical experience in the field of research writing is the cause of their reluctance. This emphasizes how urgent it is to take extensive steps to empower these teachers and provide them with the skills and confidence they need to teach practical research. Mentoring and coaching support for teachers are imperative in addressing this issue. In short, teachers were facing the challenges such as the difficulty in giving instructions and producing an output.

To address the identified issue, the researchers propose the implementation of the District Learning Action Cell (DsLAC) as an intervention. The intervention involves collaborative learning sessions where teachers can share their challenges, exchange ideas, and receive guidance on teaching practical research. By providing a supportive and collaborative environment, the intervention approach aims to build teachers' confidence and capabilities in teaching practical research subjects.

The primary objective of this study is to evaluate how the District Learning Action Cell (DsLAC) intervention can effectively address teachers' apprehension to teach practical research. The ultimate aim is to overcome any resistance or hesitations that teachers may have towards teaching this subject by providing them with the necessary knowledge and support. Through the implementation of this innovative approach, teachers in San Fernando District II will have the chance to gain valuable insights and develop their interest in teaching practices for practical research.

Action Research Question

How does the implementation of the District Learning Action Cell (DsLAC) help to alleviate teachers' apprehensions about teaching practical research subjects?

Proposed Innovation, Intervention, or Strategy

In the San Fernando II District, there is a significant issue of teachers lacking confidence in teaching the Practical Research subject. This challenge poses a barrier to providing high-quality education to students. To address this concern, the research district coordinator plans to implement the District Learning Action Cell (DsLAC) as an intervention specifically designed to alleviate teachers' apprehensions in the San Fernando II District.

Pre-Implementation Phase. During the study, several careful steps are taken. Initially, the researcher secure permission from the principal of where the researcher is affiliated, and the district supervisor. Once approval is granted, the researchers organize focus group discussions with senior high school teachers from the San Fernando II District to listen to their worries and apprehensions about teaching practical research to students. The conversation during a focus group discussion center on the teachers' reluctance to teach the subject. Following the focus group, the researcher undertakes the required preparations to implement the intervention strategy, addressing the issues and concerns collected.

Implementation Phase. As part of the devised strategy,

the researcher initiate the implementation of the District Learning Action Cell (DsLAC) to address the concerns of teachers in San Fernando II District when tasked with teaching the Practical Research subject. The DsLAC intervention encompasses collaborative learning sessions designed to alleviate apprehensions and enhance teaching practices. These sessions actively engage teachers in cooperative learning activities where they receive guidance on effective Practical Research instruction, exchange ideas, and discuss challenges they face. The primary objective is to cultivate a supportive environment that fosters knowledge-sharing, provides guidance, and collectively boosts confidence in delivering successful Practical Research lessons through mentoring and coaching.

In addition to facilitating collaborative learning sessions, the researchers ensure that research participants are well-informed about the study's objectives, parameters, and timeline. Prior to their involvement, participants are approached to secure their voluntary and informed consent, addressing any ethical considerations that may arise. This transparent approach underscores the researchers' commitment to upholding ethical standards and prioritizing the well-being and rights of the participants involved in the study.

The implementation of the strategy will be meticulously documented to capture the process, outcomes, and impact of the DsLAC intervention on teachers' confidence and instructional practices. By documenting each step of the intervention, researchers can evaluate the effectiveness of the strategy, identify areas for improvement, and gather valuable insights that can inform future interventions or adaptations. This documentation serves as a valuable tool for assessing the success of the initiative, highlighting best practices, and sharing lessons learned with stakeholders to drive continuous improvement and innovation in supporting educators in their professional development journey.

Post Implementation Phase. Following the intensive focus groups and collaborative training sessions, teachers have undergone a transformative journey, emerging with newfound confidence and enhanced skills to effectively teach the Practical Research course. Through the immersive activities facilitated by the District Learning Action Cell (DsLAC), the initial apprehensions that once plagued teachers have been alleviated, paving the way for a resurgence of self-assurance in their ability to deliver exceptional practical research instruction within the San Fernando II District. These experiences have not only bolstered their confidence but have also equipped them with the requisite knowledge and competencies essential for navigating the complexities of teaching Practical Research.

The collective wisdom and shared experiences garnered through the DsLAC activities have empowered teachers to create a more dynamic and interactive learning environment. This collaborative approach has enabled them to refine their teaching methods, explore innovative strategies, and adapt to the ever-evolving landscape of education. As a result, the professional development attained through these initiatives extends beyond individual growth, positively impacting the overall quality of practical research education throughout the district. Teachers are no longer plagued by hesitation or uncertainty when faced with the task of teaching this subject, demonstrating a newfound readiness and enthusiasm to engage their students in meaningful and effective learning experiences.

Moreover, post-implementation of the intervention, the researchers meticulously compile the outcomes of the initiatives, analyze and discuss the findings, and progress towards finalizing the report. This involves a comprehensive review of the entire body of work, subjecting it to rigorous critique and evaluation to ensure accuracy and validity. Subsequently, the research report is submitted to the research committee for the final presentation, marking the culmination of the investigative process. The dissemination and utilization of the research findings are prioritized, with the researchers presenting the outcomes and sharing actionable recommendations for practical application and further research endeavors. By disseminating these insights and recommendations, the impact of the research extends beyond the confines of the study, contributing to the broader body of knowledge and informing future educational practices and initiatives.

Chapter 2

Action Research Methods

This section thoroughly discussed the research methodology, describing the research design, the target participants, data gathering, data analysis and ethical considerations.

Research Design

This study employs a qualitative descriptive research design to explore the experiences and the challenges of the teachers during the implementation and effectiveness of the District Learning Action Cell (DsLAC) intervention in improving the teaching of practical research in schools, specifically in District 2 of San Fernando. Following Thomas' (2006) suggestion, a general inductive approach will be used to analyze the qualitative data. This technique entails systematically classifying and categorizing the data to uncover patterns and themes.

By employing this approach, the research intends to offer a thorough explanation of the DsLAC intervention's implementation process and results, aiding in the creation of focused group discussion strategies and support networks that will raise the standard of education in different schools in the San Fernando district. Additionally, the research aims to evaluate the effectiveness of the intervention on teachers' apprehensions about teaching practical research and enhance their knowledge and capabilities in this area. The findings will provide valuable insights into effective strategies for improving practical research instruction and benefit teachers in District 2 of San Fernando by equipping them with the necessary knowledge and support.

Research Participants

District Learning Action Cell (DsLAC) is an intervention to address teachers' apprehension in teaching practical research. By complete enumeration, the participants of the study included the selected senior high school teachers from San Fernando II District. Led by researcher, the San Fernando II District Research Coordinator, and committed teacher, this initiative will foster collaborative learning sessions where teachers can openly discuss their challenges, exchange creative ideas, and seek guidance on effectively instructing practical research. By involving these dedicated educators from various schools in the district, the intervention aims to provide comprehensive support and guidance in the teaching of practical research subjects.

Data Gathering Procedure

The data gathering methods of this study will follow the following phases such as pre-data collection, actual data collection and post data collection.

Pre-data Collection. The initial phase of the study involves securing all necessary permissions to conduct the research. The researchers will first seek clearance from the Research Committee. Following this, a letter will be composed and sent to the School Principal's office, requesting permission to conduct the study and obtaining permission from the District Supervisor. Subsequently, letters will be addressed to all the administrator from San Fernando II District Senior High School informing them about the research.

Actual Data Collection. The intervention, spearheaded by the Research Coordinator of San Fernando District II, focuses on addressing the prevalent issue of fear and hesitation among teachers at San Fernando District Senior High School.

The teachers voiced their apprehensions about teaching practical research due to their limited understanding and experience. In order to address this, the researchers introduced the District Learning Action Cell (DsLAC) initiative, which facilitated collaborative learning sessions where teachers could openly discuss their concerns, share ideas, and receive guidance. The researcher then conducted a comprehensive evaluation of the participants' development in teaching the intricate subject of practical research by administering a detailed questionnaire. The main objective of this questionnaire is to evaluate how much teachers have improved their confidence in teaching practical research content to their students.

Post Data Collection. Following the implementation of the District Learning Action Cell and subsequent administration of the comprehensive questionnaire, the researcher gathers the data obtained from the survey. Subsequently, employing coding analysis, the researcher interpret the gathered information. The process of data interpretation serves as the foundation for the qualitative approach utilized in presenting the findings. Through narrative descriptions, the researcher creates a compelling narrative that explains their apprehensions about teaching practical research subjects to the participants.

Data Analysis

To gain a more profound insight into the individual apprehensions and perspectives that have influenced the research outcomes, the study will leverage coding analysis. By applying the qualitative analysis method of coding, following the guidelines set by the University of Illinois, researchers can extract pertinent information from the data by delineating crucial details. This qualitative approach entails categorizing and interpreting teachers' responses to unveil their concerns and challenges in delivering practical research lessons.

This meticulous examination employs qualitative methods to pinpoint the specific apprehensions that teachers encounter when teaching practical research to students. The primary objective is to achieve a comprehensive understanding of teachers' overall effectiveness and extract valuable insights from their unique experiences contributing to this goal. This enhanced comprehension is essential for optimizing teaching outcomes for teachers and providing guidance for future enhancements in practical research education.

Furthermore, the qualitative analysis will not only identify teachers' apprehensions but also offer insights into potential solutions and strategies for improvement. By understanding the specific concerns and viewpoints of teachers, the study can propose targeted interventions and professional development opportunities to address these challenges effectively. This tailored approach can lead to enhanced teacher confidence, improved instructional practices, and ultimately, better learning outcomes for students in practical research.

Ethical Consideration

In this research study, the participants' safety and well-being are of utmost importance. When performing the study, the researcher closely followed the established protocols outlined by ethical standards and principles in order to protect the study's safety and ethical integrity.

Chapter 3

Discussion Of Results And Reflection

This chapter focused on the presentation, analysis, and interpretation of data showing a significant gap in teachers' knowledge and skills, especially in teaching Practical Research. This lack of teacher expertise caused them to fear and apprehend teaching the research subject and seriously hindered the effectiveness of education. The study provided a detailed analysis and interpretation of the collected data, as well as a thorough examination of the problems in the study.

Table 1

Teachers' Experiences and Learnings **before** the District Learning Action Cell

	Indicator	Teachers' Experiences
Before the Intervention (District Learning Action Cell	Confidence and Ineffective Knowledge Transfer	Teachers exhibited low confidence in their ability to effectively teach practical research. They struggled to facilitate student learning and foster critical thinking, often resorting to rote memorization rather than engaging students in active learning.
	Expertise in Practical Research Instruction:	Teachers demonstrated a limited understanding of practical research methodologies. They struggled to design effective lessons and lacked expertise in various research designs, data analysis techniques, and ethical considerations. Many were unfamiliar with the different stages of the research process.
	Research Proposal Development	Teachers had significant difficulty in crafting well-structured research proposals. They struggled to articulate research questions, define objectives, and justify their chosen methodologies. Many lacked the skills to create a coherent and persuasive research proposal.
	Understanding of Practical Research	Teachers had difficulty in connecting theoretical concepts to real-world scenarios and practical applications and the ability to provide relevant examples and contextualize the research investigation for students.

	Student Project Completion and Oral Defenses	Student research projects and oral defenses were often poorly executed, reflecting the teachers' lack of guidance and support. Students struggled to complete their projects to a satisfactory standard, and oral defenses were often disorganized and lacked depth. Many projects were incomplete or lacked proper formatting.
	Teacher Collaboration and Support	There was little collaboration among teachers regarding practical research instruction. Teachers lacked a supportive network to share best practices and resources, leading to isolated struggles and inconsistent teaching approaches.
	Teaching Practices	Teaching practices were inconsistent and ineffective, resulting in poor student outcomes in practical research. Teachers lacked the skills and knowledge to adapt their teaching to meet the diverse learning needs of their students.

Prior to the intervention of the District Learning Action Cell, teachers voiced notable apprehension and a lack of confidence in delivering lessons on practical research. Data showed significant unpreparedness among teachers. They demonstrated significant weaknesses in teaching practical research. They lacked confidence and struggled to effectively engage students in critical thinking, relying instead on rote learning. Their understanding of research methodologies was limited, hindering their ability to design effective lessons and create well-structured research proposals. They also lacked the skills to connect theoretical concepts to practical applications. Consequently, student projects and oral defenses were often poorly executed, reflecting a lack of teacher guidance and support. Furthermore, minimal collaboration among teachers exacerbated these challenges, leading to inconsistent and ineffective teaching practices and ultimately, poor student outcomes. The DLAC intervention was implemented to directly address these identified shortcomings.

Table 2

Teachers' Experiences and Learnings **after** the District Learning Action Cell

	Indicator	Teachers' Experiences
After the Intervention (District Learning Action Cell)	Confidence and Ineffective Knowledge Transfer	Teachers exhibited significantly increased confidence in their ability to effectively teach practical research. They demonstrated improved skills in facilitating student learning and fostering critical thinking.
	Expertise in Practical Research Instruction:	Teachers gained a profound understanding of practical research methodologies, enabling them to design and deliver effective lessons. They developed expertise in various research designs, data analysis techniques, and ethical considerations.
	Research Proposal Development	Teachers became highly proficient in crafting well-structured and compelling research proposals. They learned to clearly articulate research questions, define objectives, and justify their chosen methodologies.

	Understanding of Practical Research	Teachers acquired a more refinement and comprehensive understanding of practical research principles and applications. They were able to connect theoretical concepts to real-world scenarios and practical applications.
	Student Project Completion and Oral Defenses	The intervention resulted in a marked improvement in the quality of student research projects and oral defenses. Students successfully completed their projects, demonstrating a stronger grasp of research methods and presentation skills. The projects were completed to a high standard and submitted in a professional soft-bound format.
	Teacher Collaboration and Support	The intervention fostered a collaborative environment among teachers, enabling them to share best practices and support each other in their teaching of practical research. This collaborative spirit enhanced the overall learning experience for both teachers and students.
	Teaching Practices	The gains in teacher knowledge and skills were not temporary; the intervention resulted in sustained improvements in teaching practices, leading to better student outcomes in practical research. Teachers reported increased job satisfaction and a renewed sense of efficacy in their teaching.

After the intervention of the District Learning Action Cell, teachers demonstrated significantly improved confidence and skills in teaching practical research. They gained a profound understanding of research methodologies, enabling them to design and deliver effective lessons. Their ability to craft research proposals improved dramatically, and they developed a more comprehensive understanding of practical research principles and applications. Student research projects and oral defenses showed marked improvement in quality and execution. The intervention fostered collaboration among teachers, enhancing the overall learning experience. These gains were sustained, leading to better student outcomes and increased teacher job satisfaction.

CONCLUSION

The District Learning Action Cell (DsLAC) intervention program proved highly effective in improving research methods instruction. Teachers demonstrated significant gains in confidence, knowledge, and skills, overcoming initial anxieties and developing expertise through collaborative learning. Notably, participating teachers no longer express apprehension about teaching the subject, a testament to the program's success in boosting self-efficacy and ultimately contributing to higher-quality research methods education. Its success underscores the critical importance of ongoing support and collaborative learning environments for maximizing teacher effectiveness and improving student learning outcomes. The program's impact extends beyond individual teacher improvement, serving as a strong blueprint for professional development in specialized subjects. This model holds promise for broader application and improved educational standards within the district.

Chapter 4

Action Plan

Dissemination and Utilization Report

To successfully alleviate teachers' concerns about their apprehension in teaching practical research, the introduction of the District Learning Action Cell (DsLAC) intervention is suggested for San Fernando District II. The goal of this initiative is to provide educators with the required assistance in teaching research subjects.

To encourage teachers to adopt the DsLAC intervention, a comprehensive strategy is recommended. To start, it's important to organize training workshops underlining practical research teaching methods, incorporating engaging activities and sharing of effective strategies. Also, the creation of a peer mentorship scheme where experienced teachers can help their colleagues will foster a supportive environment. Additionally, the development of cooperative learning groups and professional advancement opportunities should be encouraged to stimulate continuous learning and skill improvement among teachers.

A variety of methods will be utilized to spread and endorse the DsLAC intervention, including mentorship and coaching. School leaders and district supervisors will be made aware of the intervention via informational meetings or briefings that emphasize its objectives and benefits. These sessions will take place during. This will be done during in-service training seminars for the teachers.

REFERENCES

Abakah, E., Widin, J. & Ameyaw, E. K. (2022, April 30). Continuing Professional Development (CPD) Practices among Basic School Teachers in the Central Region of Ghana. Retrieved from https://journals.sagepub.com/doi/full/10.1177/21582440221094597

Akomolafe, C. O. and Adesua, V. O. (2015). The Classroom Environment: A Major Motivating Factor towards High Academic Performance of Senior Secondary School Students in South West Nigeria. Retrieved from The Classroom Environment: A Major Motivating Factor...: https://files.eric.ed.gov/fulltext/EJ1086098.pdf

Bajar, J., Bajar, M., & Alarcon, E. (2021). School Learning Action Cell as a remedy to out-of-field teaching: A Case in one rural school in Southern Philippines. *International Journal of Educational Management and Innovation, 2*(3), 249-260. pdf-libre.pdf (d1wqtxts1xzle7.cloudfront.net)

Binauhan, R. C. (2019). Learning action cell implementation in the public elementary schools in the division of Cavite. *International Journal of Advanced Research and Publications, 3*(11). [PDF] Learning Action Cell Implementation In The Public Elementary Schools In The Division Of Cavite | Semantic Scholar

Cabral, J. V., & Millando, M. R. (2019). School Learning Action Cell (SLAC) Sessions and Teachers' Professional

Development in Buhaynasapa National High School. *Ascendens Asia Journal of Multidisciplinary Research Abstracts*, 3(2M). School Learning Action Cell (Slac) Sessions and Teachers' Professional Development in Buhaynasapa National High School | Ascendens Asia Journal of Multidisciplinary Research Abstracts (aaresearchindex.com)

Conde, L. A., Yazon, A. D., Tan, C. S., & Bandoy, M. M. (2023). Learning Action Cell as A Channel for Teacher's Professional Competence in Elementary Schools in the Divisions of Laguna. *Education Policy and Development*, 1(2), 40-52. Learning Action Cell as A Channel for Teacher's Professional Competence in Elementary Schools in the Divisions of Laguna | Education Policy and Development (researchsynergypress.com)

Culajara, C. J. (2023). Improving teachers' professional development through School Learning Action Cell (SLAC). *Journal of Research, Policy & Practice of Teachers and Teacher Education*, 13(1), 76-88. Improving teachers' professional development through School Learning Action Cell (SLAC) | Journal of Research, Policy & Practice of Teachers and Teacher Education (upsi.edu.my)

De Vera, J. L., DE BORJA, J. O. A. N. N. A., MARIE, A., & Orleans, A. (2020). Addressing instructional gaps in K to 12 science teaching through Learning Action Cell (LAC). *International Journal of Research Publications*, 46. Addressing Instructional Gaps in K to 12 Science Teaching Through Learning Action Cell (Lac) by Jayson L. De Vera, JOANNA MARIE A. DE BORJA, Antriman Orleans :: SSRN

Pascua, M. (2019). The Effectiveness of Learning Action Cell Sessions in Naguilian Central School. *Ascendens Asia Singapore–Union Christian College Philippines*

Journal of Multidisciplinary Research Abstracts, 2(1). The Effectiveness of Learning Action Cell Sessions in Naguilian Central School | Ascendens Asia Singapore – Union Christian College Philippines Journal of Multidisciplinary Research Abstracts (aaresearchindex.com)

Silva, V. C. (2021). School Learning Action Cell as a key for teacher's continuous learning and development. *International Journal of Research in Engineering, Science and Management, 4*(8), 12-18. School Learning Action Cell as a Key for Teacher's Continuous Learning and Development | International Journal of Research in Engineering, Science and Management (ijresm.com)

Sumbilla, C. S., Trogo, L. C. S., & Luntao, M. C. (2022). Collaborative Learning Action Cell (CLAC) mentoring program to self efficacy of the out-of-field senior high school teachers. *Indonesian Journal of Social Science, 14*(2).

Thomas, D. R. (2006). A general inductive approach for analyzing qualitative evaluation data. *American journal of evaluation, 27*(2), 237-246. A General Inductive Approach for Analyzing Qualitative Evaluation Data - David R. Thomas, 2006 (sagepub.com)

VALDEHUEZA, M. R. S., & VILLANUEVA, J. A. (2023). LEARNING ACTION CELL INSTRUCTIONAL DESIGNS AND TEACHERS'PERFORMANCE IN TALAKAG II DISTRICT. LEARNING-ACTION-CELL-INSTRUCTIONAL-DESIGNS-AND-TEACHERS-PERFORMANCE-IN-TALAKAG-II-DISTRICT.pdf (researchgate.net)VEGA, M. G. A. (2020). Investigating the learning action cell (LAC) experiences of science teachers in secondary schools: A multiple case study. *IOER Multidisciplinary Research Journal, 2*(1). Investigating the Learning Action Cell (Lac) Experiences of Science Teachers in

<u>Secondary Schools: A Multiple Case Study by MARK GIL A. VEGA :: SSRN</u>

Verbo, R. (2020). Learning Action Cell (LAC) as a School-Based Continuing Profession Development Program. In *Proceedings 25th Asian Technology Conference in Mathematics, ATCM.* <u>The Center of Gravity of Plane Regions and Ruler and Compass Constructions (mathandtech.org)</u>

APPENDICES

TRANSMITTAL LETTER
Sangat National High School
Sangat, San Fernando, Cebu

February 22, 2024

Jenelyn V. Craste
PSDS-San Fernando II
San Fernando, Cebu

Madam Craste,

Greetings!

The undersigned will be conducting an **action research study** with the title "District Learning Action Cell (DsLAC): **Intervention for Teachers' Apprehension to Teach Practical Research**" to address the apprehension among teachers in teaching practical research in San Fernando District II.

In this regard, the researchers would like to ask approval from your good office to conduct the study in different Schools in San Fernando District II. Rest assured that the documents taken from the study participants and research environment will be kept confidential.

I am looking forward for a favorable approval on this matter.

Truly yours,

CERELO B. ABASOLO
Researcher

Approved:

Jenelyn V. Craste
PSDS-San Fernando II

TRANSMITTAL LETTER
Sangat National High School
Sangat, San Fernando, Cebu

Date: February 22, 2024

NANETTE D. YMALAY, DevEdD
The Principal
Sangat National High School
Sangat, San Fernando, Cebu

THRU:
Senior High School Teachers
San Fernando District II

Madam,

Greetings!

The undersigned will be conducting an **action research study** with the title **"District Learning Action Cell (DsLAC): Intervention for Teachers' Apprehension to Teach Practical Research"** to address the apprehension among teachers in teaching practical research in San Fernando District II.

In this regard, the researchers would like to ask approval from your good office to conduct the study in different Schools in San Fernando District II. Rest assured that the documents taken from the study participants and research environment will be kept confidential.

I am looking forward for a favorable approval on this matter.

Sincerely yours,

CERELO ABASOLO
Researcher

Noted by:
NANETTE D. YMALAY, DevEdD
Principal 1

Approved by:
JENELYN V. CRASTE
PSDS- San Fernando II

Research Instruments

Instructions for Participants:

This survey aims to understand your experiences and perspectives related to teaching practices and research integration, both before and after participating in the District Learning Action Cell. Please answer each question thoughtfully and comprehensively, providing detailed responses that reflect your personal experiences. **All responses will be kept strictly confidential and will only be used for the purposes of this research study.** Your honest and detailed feedback is crucial to this qualitative research study. Thank you for your participation.

Indicator	Before Intervention	Teachers' experiences
Confidence and Ineffective Knowledge Transfer	Explain your confidence in effectively transferring knowledge to students. What challenges did you face?	
Expertise in Practical Research Instruction:	Detail your expertise in integrating practical research into your instruction. What methods or tools did you employ?	
Research Proposal Development	Illustrate your experience developing research proposals. What were the strengths and weaknesses of your approach?	
Understanding of Practical Research	Assess your understanding of practical research methods. Which aspects were you most comfortable with, and which presented challenges?	

Student Project Completion and Oral Defenses	Describe your students' experiences with completing projects and delivering oral defenses. (if applicable).	
Teacher Collaboration and Support	Explain your experiences with teacher collaboration and support.	
Teaching Practices	Discuss your teaching practices.	

Indicator	After the Intervention (District Learning Action Cell)	Teachers' experiences
Confidence and Ineffective Knowledge Transfer	Evaluate your confidence in effectively transferring knowledge to students *after* the intervention. How has your approach changed?	
Expertise in Practical Research Instruction:	Describe your expertise in integrating practical research into your instruction *after* the intervention. How has your approach evolved?	
Research Proposal Development	Assess your experience developing research proposals *after* the intervention. How has your approach improved?	
Understanding of Practical Research	Discuss your understanding of practical research methods *after* the intervention. How has your understanding deepened?	

Student Project Completion and Oral Defenses	Evaluate your students' experiences with completing projects and delivering oral defenses *after* the intervention. How did the intervention impact their performance?	
Teacher Collaboration and Support	Analyze your experiences with teacher collaboration and support *after* the intervention. How did the intervention influence your interactions with colleagues?	
Teaching Practices	Describe how your teaching practices have changed *after* the intervention. What aspects of your teaching have been most significantly altered?	

RESEARCH MANAGEMENT:
APPLICATION FORM AND ENDORSEMENT OF IMMEDIATE SUPERVISOR(S) OF THE PROPONENT(S) TEMPLATE

A. RESEARCH INFORMATION

TITLE OF ACTION RESEARCH
District Learning Action Cell (DsLAC): Intervention for Teachers' Apprehension to Teach Practical Research
SHORT DESCRIPTION OF THE RESEARCH
In San Fernando District II, the noble aim of education encounters a significant challenge as teachers lack confidence and feel hesitant about teaching practical research subjects. To tackle this issue, the researcher implements the District Learning Action Cell (DsLAC) intervention. This initiative entails collaborative learning sessions where teachers can openly discuss their difficulties, exchange insights, and receive guidance on teaching practical research. By fostering a supportive and collaborative atmosphere, the intervention aims to bolster teachers' confidence and capabilities in delivering practical research course.

RESEARCH AGENDA CATEGORY	

(Please check <u>only one</u>)
Main Themes
1. Teaching and Learning
    ___ a. Instruction
    ___ b. Curriculum
    ___ c. Learners
    ___ d. Assessment
    ___ e. Learning Outcomes
2. Child Protection
    ___ a. Bullying
    ___ b. Teenage Pregnancy
    ___ c. Child Abuse
    ___ d. Addiction
    ___ e. Media Consumption
3. Human Resource Development
    ___ a. Teaching and Non-Teaching
          Qualifications and Hiring
    ___ b. Career Development
    ___ c. Employee Welfare
4. Governance
    ___ a. Planning
    ___ b. Finance
    ___ c. Program Management
    ___ d. Transparency and
          Accountability
    ___ e. Evaluation
	(Please check any, if applicable)
	Cut-Across Themes
	1. Disaster Risk Reduction and
	    Management (DRRM)
	    ___ a. Prevention and Mitigation
	    ___ b. Preparedness
	    ___ c. Response
	    ___ d. Rehabilitation and Recovery
	___ 2. Gender and Development (GAD)
	___ 3. Inclusive Education
	___ 4. Others (please specify): _____
	
	--- 	
	
	RESEARCH SCOPE
	(please check <u>only one</u>)
	    ___ National
	    ___ Region
	    ___ Division
	    ___ District
	    ___ School
	
	RESEARCH CATEGORY
	(please check <u>only one</u>)
	    ___ **Action Research**
	    ___ **Basic Research**

FUND SOURCE (e.g. BERF, SEF, others)*	**AMOUNT**
TOTAL AMOUNT	

RESEARCH MANAGEMENT:
DECLARATION OF ANTI-PLAGIARISM

1. I ,Cerelo B. Abasolo , understand that plagiarism is the act of taking and using another's ideas and works and passing them off as one's own. This includes explicitly copying the whole work of another person and/or using some parts of such work without proper acknowledgement and referencing

2. We hereby attest to the originality of this research proposal and has/ have cited properly all the references used. I/We further commit that all deliverables and the final research study emanating from this proposal shall be of original content. I/We shall use appropriate citations in referencing other works from various sources.

3. We understand that violation from this declaration and commitment shall be subject to consequences and shall be dealt with accordingly by the Department of Education, as stipulated in DO. No. 16, s 2017 entitled "Research Management Guidelines (RMG)."

	Lead Proponent	Second Proponent	Third Proponent
Full Name	Cerelo B. Abasolo		
Position / Designation	Teacher 3		
School / District / Office	Sangat National High School-San Fernando II District		
Signature			
Date	February 22, 2024		

RESEARCH MANAGEMENT:
DECLARATION OF ABSENCE OF CONFLICT OF INTEREST

1. I, Cerelo B. Abasolo, understand that conflict of interest refers to situations in which financial or other personal considerations may compromise my/our judgement in evaluating, conducting, or reporting research.
2. We hereby declare that I/We do not have any personal conflict of interest that may arise from my/our application and submission of my/our research proposal. I/We understand that my/our research proposal may be returned to me/us if found out that there is conflict of interest during the initial screening as per item A(*ii*), Section V(B) of the Research Management Guidelines.
3. Further, in case of any form of conflict of interest (possible or actual) which may inadvertently emerge during the conduct of my/our research. I/We will duly report it to the research committee for immediate action.
4. We understand that I/We may be held accountable by the Department of Education and   (insert grant mechanism) for any conflict of interest which I/We have intentionally concealed.

	Lead Proponent	*Second Proponent*	*Third Proponent*
Full Name	Cerelo B. Abasolo		
Position / Designation	Teacher 3		
Division / District / School/ Unit/ Office	Sangat National High School-San Fernando II District		
Signature			
Date	February 22, 2024		

WORK PLANS AND TIMELINES FOR RESEARCH IMPLEMENTATION

Proponent: **Cerelo B. Abasolo**

Title of Action Research:

<u>District Learning Action Cell (DsLAC): Intervention for Teachers' Apprehension to Teach Practical Research</u>

TASKS / ACTIVITIES	TARGET DATE	PERSON(s) RESPONSIBLE / INVOLVED
Pre-Implementation Phase		
1. Researchers ask consent from the district supervisor and the principal of Sangat National High School, which is the researcher's affiliated institution and informed consent and address other ethical concerns.	January 28,2024	Researchers, Principal & School Heads , Public district supervisor
2. The researchers orients the senior high school teachers in San Fernando II, particularly those handling research subjects.	February 8,,2024	Researchers, School Heads, School Research coordinator, Teacher
3. Researchers conducted a focus group discussion with the senior high school teachers in San Fernando II District to identify their concerns about teaching the Practical Research subject.	February 23,,2024	Researchers, Research coordinator, Teachers

Implementation Phase		
1. Researchers takes the lead and puts the District Learning Action Cell (DsLAC) into action.	February 27,March 1, 8,15,22,29,- April 5 ,12 ,19,26, 2024	Researchers, School Heads, School Research coordinator, Teachers
2. Teachers take an active part in cooperative learning exercises. They get advice on how to effectively teach the Practical Research course, share ideas, and discuss the difficulties they have encountered.	February 27,March 1, 8,15,22,29,- April 5 ,12 ,19,26, 2024	Researchers, Research coordinator, Teachers
3. The researchers informs the research participants about the goals, parameters, and timeline of the study. Secures their voluntary and informed consent and addresses other ethical concerns.	February 27,March 1, 8,15,22,29,- April 5 ,12 ,19,26, 2024	Researchers, Research coordinator, Teachers
Post Implementation Phase		
1. The Researchers consolidate the results; tally and compute the data using the appropriate statistical tools.	February 27,March 1, 8,15,22,29,- April 5 ,12 ,19,26, 2024	Researchers

Certification that the output of the research has been implemented by the research duly issued by the Head of Office

COST ESTIMATES FOR RESEARCH IMPLEMENTATION
(Action Research)

Title of Action Research:

District Learning Action Cell (DsLAC): Intervention for Teachers' Apprehension to Teach Practical Research

ACTIVITIES / CATEGORIES	RESOURCES / MATERIALS	ESTIMATED COST	TOTAL
Conduct of an Action Research	Short Bond paper	160.00	1,280.00
Writing an Action Research	Long Bond paper	185.00	1,480.00
Conduct a Focus group Discussion (Day 1-7)	12 pax Snacks	50.00	4,200.00
Conduct of an Action Research Printing	Epson 003 Ink	390.00	1,560.00
TOTAL FIRST TRANCHE		Sub-total	Php 4,800.00
SECOND TRANCHE			
Printing	Short Bondpaper	185.00	185.00
		Sub-total	185.00
TOTAL TRANCHES			Php 4,985.00

Prepared by:
CERELO B. ABASOLO
Lead Proponent
Name & Signature

Date:

Certified Correct:
NANETTE D. YAMALAY, DevEd.D
Lead Proponent's Immediate Supervisor

IMMEDIATE SUPERVISOR'S CONFORME

I hereby endorse the attached **CLASSROOM-BASED ACTION RESEARCH COMPLETED.** I certify that the proponent/s has/have the capacity to conduct a research study without compromising his/her/their office functions.

	Lead Proponent's Immediate Supervisor	Second Proponent's Immediate Supervisor	Third Proponent's Immediate Supervisor
Full Name	Nanette D. Ymalay, DevEdD		
Position / Designation	Principal 1		
School / District / Office (SDO/FD)	Sangat NHS		
Signature			
Date	February 22, 2024		

PROPONENT INFORMATION
LEAD PROPONENT / INDIVIDUAL PROPONENT

LAST NAME: Abasolo	FIRST NAME: Cerelo	MIDDLE NAME: Barolo

BIRTHDATE (MM/DD/YYYY) 02/09/1979	SEX: ☑ Male ☐ Female	POSITION Teacher 3
		DESIGNATION: (if applicable) District research coordinator

CONTACT NUMBER 1: 0997710036	CONTACT NUMBER 2:	EMAIL ADDRESS: cerelo.abasolo@deped.gov.

NAME OF SCHOOL / DISTRICT / OFFICE ASSIGNED Sangat National High School	CONTACT NUMBER OF SCHOOL / DISTRICT / OFFICE	
ADDRESS OF SCHOOL / DISTRICT / OFFICE ASSIGNED Sangat, San Fernando ,Cebu	DIVISION Cebu	REGION VII

EDUCATIONAL ATTAINMENT (DEGREE TITLE) *enumerate from bachelor's degree up to doctorate degree*	TITLE OF THESIS / RELATED RESEARCH PROJECT Enhancing Learners' Physics Performance through Science Club Integration

EDUCATIONAL ATTAINMENT (DEGREE TITLE) *enumerate from bachelor's degree up to doctorate degree*	TITLE OF THESIS / RELATED RESEARCH PROJECT
SIGNATURE OF PROPONENT:	

RESEARCH MANAGEMENT:
RESEARCH PROPONENT(S) PROFILE

Last Name:	**Abasolo**
First Name:	**Cerelo**
Middle Name:	**Barolo**
Sex:	**Male**
Date of Birth:	**February 9, 1979**
DepEd Email Address:	cerelo.abasolo@deped.gov.ph

Personal Background

Current Address:	Tubod, San Fernando, Cebu
Provincial Address:	Tubod, San Fernando, Cebu
Contact Number 1:	09977100361
Contact Number 2:	
Bachelor Degree/s:	B.S General Science

Number of Years in DepEd:	11 years and 3 months	Number of BERF/ Non-BERF Researches:	

Work Information:

Region:	VII	Division:	Cebu Province
Position:	Teacher 3	Designation: (If Applicable)	District Research Coordinator
Name of School / District / Office assigned:	Sangat National High School-San Fernando II District	Name of Immediate Superior:	Nanette D. Ymalay, DevEd.D
Address of School / District / Office assigned:	Sangat, San Fernando, Cebu	Contact number of School / District / Office:	
Email Address of Immediate Superior:		Contact Number of Immediate Superior:	

Major Accomplishments: [for the last Three (3) Years

	Related Trainings Conducted
1	Division Action Research training workshop
2	Division Basic Research Training workshop

	Awards / Recognition Received
1	Regional Research Presenter/ Choose as Regional Virtual Summit Presenter
2	District Research Awardee

Republic of the Philippines

Department of Education
REGION VII, CENTRAL VISAYAS
SCHOOLS DIVISION OF CEBU PROVINCE
DISTRICT OF SAN FERNANDO II
San Fernando, Cebu

San Fernando II District Learning Action Cell (DsLAC) for
Teachers teaching Practical Research/ Action Research

1st (DsLAC Session)

Republic of the Philippines

Department of Education
REGION VII, CENTRAL VISAYAS
SCHOOLS DIVISION OF CEBU PROVINCE
DISTRICT OF SAN FERNANDO II
San Fernando, Cebu

San Fernando II District Learning Action Cell (DsLAC) for
Teachers teaching Practical Research/ Action Research

2nd (DsLAC Session)

Republic of the Philippines

Department of Education
REGION VII, CENTRAL VISAYAS
SCHOOLS DIVISION OF CEBU PROVINCE
DISTRICT OF SAN FERNANDO II
San Fernando, Cebu

San Fernando II District Learning Action Cell (DsLAC) for
Teachers teaching Practical Research/ Action Research

3rd (DsLAC Session)

San Fernando II District Learning Action Cell (DsLAC) for Teachers teaching Practical Research/ Action Research

4th (DsLAC Session)

Republic of the Philippines

Department of Education

REGION VII, CENTRAL VISAYAS
SCHOOLS DIVISION OF CEBU PROVINCE
DISTRICT OF SAN FERNANDO II
San Fernando, Cebu

San Fernando II District Learning Action Cell (DsLAC) for Teachers teaching Practical Research/ Action Research

5th (DsLAC Session)

San Fernando II District Learning Action Cell (DsLAC) for Teachers teaching Practical Research/ Action Research

6th (DsLAC Session)

Republic of the Philippines

Department of Education
REGION VII, CENTRAL VISAYAS
SCHOOLS DIVISION OF CEBU PROVINCE
DISTRICT OF SAN FERNANDO II
San Fernando, Cebu

San Fernando II District Learning Action Cell (DsLAC) for
Teachers teaching Practical Research/ Action Research

7th (DsLAC Session)

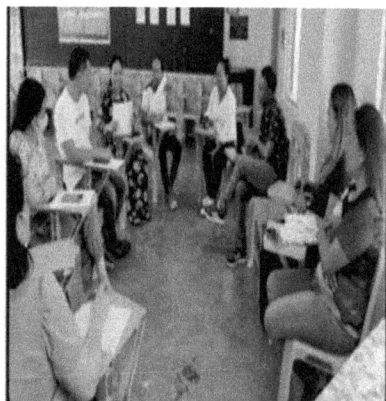

www.ingramcontent.com/pod-product-compliance
Lightning Source LLC
Chambersburg PA
CBHW032103020426
42335CB00011B/474